Soaring above the Silent Enemy

To: Tina

May God bless you
love
B. Dixon

Soaring above the Silent Enemy

Victory Is on the Horizon

by

Brenda L. Wilson

DORRANCE PUBLISHING CO., INC.
PITTSBURGH, PENNSYLVANIA 15222

As indicated, Scripture is taken from the Holy Bible, King James Version, and the Holy Bible, New International Version. Please note that all quoted Scripture has been *italicized*.

The name of satan is not in capital letters; the emphasis of the author is to glorify and honor the Lord Jesus.

Scripture taken from the HOLY BIBLE, NEW INTERNATIONAL VERSION®. Copyright © 1973, 1978, 1984 by International Bible Society. Used by permission of Zondervan Publishing House. All rights reserved.

The "NIV" and "New International Version" trademarks are registered in the United States Patent Office by International Bible Society. Use of either trademark requires permission of International Bible Society.

All Rights Reserved
Copyright © 2003 by Brenda Wilson
No part of this book may be reproduced or transmitted
in any form or by any means, electronic or mechanical,
including photocopying, recording, or by any informational
storage and retrieval system without permission in
writing from the publisher.

ISBN #0-8059-5902-5
Printed in the United States of America

First Printing

For information or to order additional books, please write:
Dorrance Publishing Co., Inc.
701 Smithfield Street
Third Floor
Pittsburgh, Pennsylvania 15222
U.S.A.
1-800-788-7654
Or visit our web site and on-line catalog at www.dorrancepublishing.com

This book is dedicated to my four wonderful children:
DeAngela, Stephino, Antoinette, and Brandon.

Chapter Outline

Chapter One: The Silent Enemy—Stress
Defines the silent enemy as stress. Factors are discussed that cause stress. Readers are given a self-inventory that evaluates their emotional state.

Chapter Two: Facing the Problems That Cause Stress
Examines the various avenues of stress: emotions, American families, women's issues.

Chapter Three: Making the Correct Choices
Discussion on the spiritual decisions we make that cause stress in our Christian walk.

Chapter Four: The Challenges
Presents case problems of typical families who are going through various challenges. The reader is encouraged to develop potential outcomes. At the end of each case, Biblical solutions are offered.

Chapter Five: Mental and Physical Effects
Examines the physical and mental effects of stress. Discusses identifying warning signs, getting qualified help, letting go of hang up, healing of emotions, and getting rid of excuses.

Chapter Six: Spiritual Warfare
Biblical truths are presented that define our enemy. Examines his characteristics and purpose of attack. Case problems are presented that illustrate the various areas in which satan attacks our lives. The chapter ends proclaiming victory in Jesus's Name.

Chapter Seven: Soaring Above the Enemy
Discusses preparing for strategic warfare. A non-exhaustive listing of demonic strong holds and their lesser demons are given. Case problems that illustrate the topic are presented along with biblical truths.

Chapter Eight: Challenges of the Ministry
Dedicated to women in the ministry. Discusses the problems and challenges faced both in the home and ministry. Presents a proposed time management schedule to help organize the day.

Chapter Nine: Problem to Recovery
Discusses the areas in our lives that are hindrances to full recovery. Suggestions are offered to alleviate the amount of stress through proper diet, health, time management, exercise, and forgiveness. The reader is encouraged to keep a log of those areas that cause stress.

Foreword

This book represents a message of hope to the women of God who are suffering from fear, despair, depression, suicidal thoughts, compulsive behaviors, and anger.

Many women are ashamed to admit they are stressed out because of beliefs held by many within the Christian body. This book offers biblical truths and examples of how the people of old also faced distress. I have illustrated how some of the old saints doubted God's ability to deliver them and others declared boldly that God was their very present help in the time of trouble.

Simulated case problems along with my own personal experience are offered to help the women of God evaluate their emotional reactions to others' demands and arrive at possible solutions to their own personal situations. The book evaluates factors causing stress and offers solutions for controlling the emotions.

The women of God are encouraged to take a stand against every wile of the devil by using the creative Word of God. The Word of God assures the believer that heaven has declared victory in all areas of their lives.

Acknowledgments

My deepest appreciation is to the Lord and Savior Jesus Christ who has inspired me to write this book.

I want to thank my two beautiful daughters, DeAngela and Antoinette, for listening to me read my drafts and giving helpful insights.

To the Women's Department of Philadelphia Church, thanks for allowing me to present my stress management class to you. Many of you were blessed and encouraged by these seminars.

Casting Our Cares Upon Him

Dear Sister:

How are you? I just had to send this letter to tell you how much I care about you.

I saw you yesterday as you desperately tried to solve many problems. I waited for you to cast your cares upon me, for I care for you.

My sister, I watched as you tossed and turned in your bed all night. I thought, surely she will allow me to work it out. I carried the griefs, despairs, pains, illnesses, and needs of the whole world and nailed them to the cross.

Ask me, and I will speak to the raging storms in your life and command them to be still.

Come unto me all ye that are laden and heavy burdened, and I will give you rest.

Your friend,
Jesus

Chapter One
The Silent Enemy: Stress

What is Stress?
Webster defines stress as an "emotional, physical, or chemical factor that causes bodily or mental tension."

Stress is our internal reaction to things that happen to us and demands that are placed on us. Stress results from both negative and positive experiences in our lives. Negative stress occurs when we are worried, afraid, angered, ashamed, or anxious. Further, experiences such as depression, fear, arguments, divorce, death, and exhaustion open the door to stress. Positive stress can result from experiences such as graduation, promotions, birth of a child, or marriage. An individual who is coping with life threatening or prolonged illness can experience stress.

Environmental factors can also heighten or lessen stress levels. For example, a warm sunny day may elicit a positive inner feeling. On the other hand, a cloudy day may elicit a negative inner feeling. According to recent studies, stress is considered the number one killer in our country today. Individuals who are likely to suffer from strokes, high blood pressure, or heart attacks are more prone to severe panic attacks.

Spiritual warfare is another area in which Christians will be faced with stress. Being spiritually prepared through prayer, fasting, and having on the armor of God is the best defense against demonic attacks.

Stress operates against the peace God has guaranteed to every believer. The Bible instructs the believer not to let the heart be fearful of circumstances.

Stress can be dealt with adequately only when we learn how to handle the external events and demands and control our internal reaction to them.

Response to Stress

Any external stimuli that triggers some type of emotional response can cause stress. This is known as the stressor response. Often people limit their view of stress to the stressor. The stressor is identified as how we view the actions of other people and demands we feel are placed on our actions.

The stressor will not always have the same effect on different individuals. The stressor effect will vary depending on the individual's reaction to what is happening. For example, a traffic jam may heighten the adrenaline level for one person while on the other hand, sitting in the traffic may have little or no effect on the next person. Stress can only occur when internal reactions to external factors cause discomfort.

External factors are not the only demands placed on us. Often we place high demands on our selves because we feel others expect more out of us. A working mother may be compelled after a day's work to clean house, cook, do laundry, shop, iron, etc. This mother may be compulsively driven to accomplish these tasks because she feels her family expects this. Her internal reaction to what she feel others are demanding can manifest into fatigue, body aches, insomnia, tension, anger, or resentment. Setting realistic expectations will help to lessen this type of stress.

Our bodies also respond to stress levels. When we become excited, glands located just below the kidneys secrete extra adrenal hormones. When these hormones are released into the blood, the body responds by an elevation in blood pressure and heart rate. You may also experience sweaty palms, blurred vision, or an upset stomach if you are experiencing fear. Once the hormone level is increased, the brain then transmits a message through the motor nerves to the muscles in the arms and legs, this message says, POTENTIAL DANGER OR EXCITEMENT, PREPARE TO RESPOND.

Personal Stress Inventory

The following is a list of potentially stressful events/demands. Take a thoughtful moment to read the list and then place a mental check mark in the appropriate column that best describes your emotional state. The list is not intended to be all inclusive.

Stress Inventory

Questions	Yes	No
1. When financial problems arise, do you try to avoid your creditors?		
2. Do you have difficulty saying 'I cannot meet deadlines' because of prior commitments?		

3. Do you feel tired the next morning even after a night's sleep?

4. For no apparent reason, have you ever suffered from attacks of fear?

5. Are you easily agitated when you do not know how to respond to a request?

6. Do you make excuses in order to avoid making decisions?

7. Are you over self-sacrificing?

8. When faced with problems, do you suffer from attacks of unaccountable headaches?

9. Do you ever withdraw from people or family?

10. Do you ever cry for no apparent reason?

11. Have you ever suffered from physical or mental abuse?

12. Do you have thoughts of suicide?

If you answered yes to any of the above questions, you are a prime candidate for stress or you are already suffering from stress.

Stress not only attacks us personally, it reaches out with invisible arms and enfolds others in our immediate environment. It leaves a path strewn with arguments, abuse, denial, neglect, broken hearts, lack of communication, and destroyed relationships.

Controlling Your Stress Level
Each day you are going to encounter both external and internal demands and events that will affect your emotional state. Although you cannot control the actions of others, you can take charge of your own actions and thoughts. Let's look at an external stressor that most of us are familiar with: your typical morning traffic jam.

You are sitting in a traffic jam on a hot afternoon. You're thinking, *I'm late for a very important meeting and this is going to cost me this contract.* How would you respond to this situation? Suppose you opt to repeatedly blow your horn or yell at the driver in front of you. One possible effect this would have is to antagonize other drivers and increase your own anxiety level. The other possible choice would be for you to turn on your music and patiently wait the situation out. By following this path, you create an atmosphere of peace within yourself. Further, you have lowered your stress level and may also be able to find ways to win the contract.

An example of an internal conflict might be a feeling of panic after studying all night for a final exam. You are sure you will not recall anything you have studied. What should you do? Take a moment to say a prayer before starting your day. Ask the Lord to restore your self-confidence and help you to relax during the exam. God works miracles.

When both external and internal stressors are out of control, the Word of God is the only effective weapon you have to restore your peace of mind. The Bible instructs the believer to guard the thought process by thinking *on "good things, things of good report, things that are pure and honest and things that bring harmony and peace."* As you begin to guard your thought process, you will find your stress level decreasing. You will also experience more peace in your life. In the book of Isaiah, the Lord promises to keep us in perfect peace if the heart and mind are focused on him.

Fretting and worrying about conditions we cannot control is a sin. Matthew 6 emphasizes God's provincial care over creation and man. He is concerned about your needs, desires, hurts, despairs, pressures, health, and economic well being. With such a loving God caring and providing for us there is no room to become **stressed out.**

Chapter Two
Facing the Problems Causing Stress

The road to recovery is often lonely and full of despair. The lone traveler must possess self-determination to strive for the help and healing needed despite the obstacles.

Admitting the Problem
A few years ago, I was involved in an outreach ministry that worked with recovering drug and alcohol addicts. I noted each meeting had the same agenda; some grateful soul would mount the platform and proclaim to their peers, "I have a problem, I am an alcoholic." I pondered their statement for a while. Why should a recovered addict still proclaim addiction? Why not say, "I used to be an alcoholic, but now I have amended my ways?" After I had observed this ritual for several meetings, the answer finally hit me. The key to recovery is in admitting you have a problem and need help. Stress left unchecked is a problem that leads to both physical and mental breakdowns. Every person—without regard to social status, gender, or religious affiliation—is prone to attacks of stress.

Problems Coping With Your Emotions
Webster defines the emotions as any strong, generalized feelings, physical excitement; any of various complex reactions with both mental and physical manifestations; as love, hate, fear, anger, etc.

The biblical definition refers to it as the mind (*skua* in Greek), the seat of our thinking/intellect. The believer is warned that the thinking process should be renewed daily and that evil thoughts are sins. "*So as a man thinketh in his heart, so is he.*" It is not what we consume daily that defiles us; it is what comes from the thinking process that defiles our actions.

Chapter One discussed external, internal, and environmental factors that heighten or lessen the amount of stress you felt. Stress can be dealt with only by understanding the real motives of others and controlling your own thought process. We have been given the spirit of discernment by which we are able to try the spirits by the spirit of God. When we take responsibility for our reactions to the stressor, we will be able to control the amount of stress we are experiencing. Perceiving negative demands/actions may cause you to react in like manner if your emotions are not subject to the will of God.

Misunderstanding the intents and actions of others leads to strife, resentment, anger, broken relationships, and miscommunication. It is therefore important that the believer, through Godly wisdom, guard their emotions. When the emotions are subject to the will of God, our reactions to any stressor will lead to peace and harmony.

I remember when I was struggling to maintain a career, manage a home, and complete degree work all at the same time. I recall feeling others were placing demands on my life that I was not capable of measuring up to. The more I struggled to meet demands, the more stressed I became. I began experiencing negative feelings both towards others and my inability to measure up to what I was perceiving. When I began to seek the Lord's guidance, Proverbs 3 came to mind, *"In all thy getting, get an understanding."* Through the guidance of the holy spirit, I was able to work out a plan that was acceptable for day-to-day tasks. My employer at that time agreed to a flex-time work schedule that allowed me to attend school at a more convenient time. Not all internal or external demands will work out smoothly; nevertheless, put forth the effort. Above everything else, prayerfully guard the loins of your mind and use wisdom. The adversary seeks to distort and bring confusion to your thought process. If you confess to God in prayer your inability to control your emotions, He is more than able to help you become victorious.

Troubled Society
There are challenges facing our society that no law, regulation, or agency can fix. These challenges are progressively growing worse with the passage of time. The Bible declares these are perilous times. I do not intend to paint a bleak picture of our society, yet the nation's only hope is to return unto the Lord with the whole heart. The nation returning unto the Lord will bring the promised blessings back into our homes.

There isn't a family who is not affected by one or more of the following stressful conditions. Many families live under the constant fear of financial disaster due to lay off, recession and credit card spending. Agencies, such as Welfare and Social Security that many look to for help are now threatening to disband due to limited funds. Teenage pregnancy is at an all time high. Young mothers are forced to abandon their educational pursuits and end up as welfare statistics. Drug and gang affiliation is the trend of the inner city youth. Drug and gang violence is the leading cause of death among our youth today. Divorce rates are on a steady incline. Even in the Christian community, divorce is viewed as the only solution to troubled family conditions. When homes are divided, the church, community, and society will also be divided. The Bible states a *"home divided against itself cannot stand."*

Women's Issues
I grew up in the era when women were burning their bras and demanding equal pay for equal work. We were finally granted the right to compete for jobs and promotions that were once considered taboo. Many women left the comforts of the home and obtained employment. Others returned back to school in order to compete for higher management positions. In the excitement of the moment, we could purchase and charge without our husbands' approval. Women, what we were not prepared for was the new levels of stress. Even though we made economic advancements, we were still accountable for the upkeep of home and family. Let's face it, even in this era of technological advancement we still spend countless hours outside the home perfecting our skills and meeting the ever increasing challenges of the workplace. To add to this, we are expected to balance into our already busy routines social activities, worship, and family obligations.

I am by no means suggesting women forfeit the challenges of their various professions. What we must do is prayerfully admit we have a problem. The addict willingly admits addition to drugs or alcohol. Christian women, we should not be ashamed to admit when we, too, are stressed out.

Chapter Three
Making the Correct Choices

Life is full of choices. The wise and prudent exercise wisdom and bring every thought and action under submission. The unwise, on the other hand, respond to the negativity of others in a like manner.

Examples of Courage
The Bible contains many narratives of the people of God being faced with despair, persecution, hunger, ill health, and life-threatening situations. They could have chosen to rely on their own abilities to better the situation or their own strength to overcome their enemies. Because their faith was toward an unfailing God, they knew he was with them in the fiery furnaces; he stood as a shield before the hungry lions; he was a mighty weapon against Goliath and the Philistine; and he was more than able to bring down the Jericho Wall.

David the Patriot is an example of a person who was not quick to respond on emotions. When faced with trouble, he looked to God rather than to his own skills. David was well acquainted with anxiety. Many years of his life were spent running from King Saul and later his own son, Absalom. Out of his distress he cried to God, *"O Lord, many are my foes. How many rise up against me. Many are saying of me, God will not deliver him."* In Psalms 10:1 he continues *"Why oh Lord, do you stand far off? Why do you hide yourself in times of trouble?"* Even though David faced many challenges and threats against his life, he yet declared his hope in God. Psalms 18:6 says, *"In my distress I called to the Lord; from his temple he heard my voice; my cry came before him, into his ears."* David knew beyond a shadow of doubt that God was his sovereign protector. Psalms 27 reflects this, *"When my enemies and foes come upon me to feat of my flesh, they shall stumble and fall. Even when a host encamps against me, my heart shall not fear, though wars should rise against me, in this will I be confident."* Instead of moping in self pity, David turns his attention from himself and begins to praise and worship God.

Choosing the Path of Doubt
Doubt is defined as: unbelief, uncertain, to wonder, indecision, to question, or dejection. Waiting on God requires the believer to have unmovable faith. Giving in to negative thoughts leads to doubt. Once doubt has set in, it hinders God from moving on your behalf.

In the narrative of the exodus from Egypt, the Children of Israel faced many stressful challenges. Nevertheless, they had the provincial care and promised deliverance of God on their side. With so much hope in sight, they still wavered in their faith toward God. With narrowed spiritual vision, they saw only the pursuit of the Egyptian army and a raging sea before them. Their doubting led to stress. Once stress set in, their thoughts and actions reflected doubt. In this state they declared, *"It was better to remain in bondage than to face the uncertainties of the hour."*

The blessed assurance we can rely on is that God is always faithful in spite of our disbelief.

Choosing the Path of Faith
Faith is defined as an "Unquestionable belief in God, complete trust, confidence, or reliance."

The narrative of Job reflects trust and belief in God's unfailing word. Job's life demonstrated love and concern for his fellow man. Job gave to the poor and needy; he made daily penance for his family; he was also a man of great honor and wisdom. Socially and economically, Job had the best that life could offer. Could a man with so much going for himself become a victim of stress? The answer is yes.

As the story of Job's life unfolds, he is stripped of his worldly possessions and health. His wife nags him to curse God and die as a way to end his misery. The lives of his children are also cut off.

Trouble attacked Job without prior warning. I'm sure Job did not attribute his trouble to any sin within his life. The Bible stated that *"He was a perfect and upright man that feared God."* I'm also sure Job was not aware that his battle was spiritual rather than the result of any mismanagement of his personal affairs. Yet his spiritual and moral walk did not exempt him from trouble.

Recall the devil went before God to report his activities. He stated, *"I'm going to and fro in the earth seeking whom I may devour."* God had such confidence in Job's faith, he directed the devil's attention to him. God challenged the devil to consider his servant Job. Job is immediately placed on the devil's hit list with one stipulation: he could not touch Job's soul. Demon forces are then assigned to torment Job's life in various forms.

Job's faith was challenged to the point where it would have been easier to curse and blame God for his problems. There were moments when remorse took hold of him and he questioned his purpose for being born. Through all this, Job yet retains his integrity. He declared, *"Naked came I out of my mother's wound, naked shall I return there. The Lord gave, and the Lord hath taken away, blessed be the name of the Lord."*

How would you have responded to such a great loss? Would you yield to despair or denial? As a believer you must understand, *"The devil comes to steal, kill and to destroy."*

Stress and the Christian Walk

You may be currently experiencing a storm in your life and wondering how you, a believer, can be suffering? You may even quote a number of Scriptures to reinforce the fact that you have laid your cares upon Jesus and any discomfort you are momentarily experiencing is not of God. Your salvation is not a guarantee of a trouble free life. In fact, just because you are a child of God makes you a prime candidate for stress. The decision to react or hold your peace marks your life as a believer. Remember, you are a light through which the world sees Jesus. When you react to others' negative demands you bring a reproach against the body of Christ. When you hold your peace, the body of Christ is edified.

The Lord promised to lift up a standard against every force of the enemy that shall come against you both spiritually and naturally. There is no weapon that will ever be formed against you that shall prosper.

Waiting on God to work out all situations that may cause discomfort requires that you to develop patience. Patience is a virtue that must have its perfect work in our lives. As we develop patience, we mature in God. Patience helps bind stressful thoughts and actions.

Take a stand and know you are not a victim to personal problems or demands of others. You are an overcomer through Jesus Christ. Don't lean on your own understanding in the time of crisis. You have the right to gain all your strength from the Lord. As a believer, boldly proclaim, *"I am more than a conqueror through Jesus Christ."*

Many of you right now are going through needless stress because you are not standing on the Word of God. The devil is aware that when you begin to put God's Word to the test he is in trouble. God's Word is so powerful that it is never sent out void, but it shall accomplish all God's purposes. Heaven and Earth shall surely dissolve, but the Word of God shall yet stand fast.

Since you, the believer, have the creative Word of God within you, speak to your troubles. Declare, "I have the victory over the spirit of depression, fear, doubt, anxiety, illness, loneliness, despair, etc. The joy of the Lord is my strength to endure. I refuse to spend another night worrying about my rent and other bills. My Father created the world and everything in it belongs to him. I am an heir of a King. I'm not sick because I have been made whole by the stripes of Jesus at Calvary." As you have spoken these words of faith, God shall bring it to pass.

I pray even now that God will build a shield of fire all around you. I bind every tormenting demon now in Jesus's name. Bring peace and rest to every heart now, Oh God. I command, in Jesus's name, the warring angels of God to go forth into battle on behalf of this dear sister. I thank you, Lord God, in advance. Amen.

I want you to realize, my sister, that problems that cause stress in your life may or may not be self-induced. Use every problem as an opportunity not a pitfall. Let Psalms 23 be of comfort to you. *"Yea though I walk through the valley of the shadow of death, I will fear no evil, for thou art with me; thy rod and they staff they comfort me...."* As you proceed patiently through each storm in your life, you can have the assurance that Jesus, God's answer to all your problems, desires to destroy every yoke and bring total healing to your emotions.

Stress and Friendship
There is an old adage that misery loves company. Many stressed out souls seek unwise comfort and counsel from well-meaning friends. In the Bible Job had three such friends who made their house call to comfort him in his hour of grief and misfortune. Instead of the warmth and comforting words expected, Job is charged as having a flaw in his character that brought the hand of a merciful God against him in wrath. Job is thus placed in an uncomfortable situation where he must justify the calamities that have befallen him. How many times have others look with disdain on your misfortunes as some punishment from God for some unconfessed sin? Has what they said about you or their actions caused stress in your life? Never feel you must justify trouble in your life to well meaning friends who unleash a load of guilt on you. Learn how to listen for the voice of comfort that can only come from God as you seek His directions.

Chapter Four
The Challenges

The opposite of stress is peace and total reliance upon the Word of God. The Bible declares, in spite of the perilous times in which we live, *Peace, I leave with you, my peace, I give unto you; not as the world giveth, give I unto you. Let not your heart be troubled, neither let it be afraid."* Woman of God, you have been given the right antidote to stress. All that is required of you is to claim your peace just as you would take a vitamin each day for your physical well-being. Remember, *"God has not given you the spirit of fear, but of power, and love, and of a sound mind."*

The following scenarios are provided that you may understand the various avenues through which stress can enter. Prayerfully think through how you would handle each case. I have also given possible solutions to each case.

Case A
You are a single mother of three lovely children. You work a job that doesn't pay enough to make ends meet.

You have just received your paycheck. The rent is due; you are low on food; your utilities are past due, and please don't forget, you owe God 10 percent.

Every born again believer must obey the Word of God concerning tithing. The question is posed, "Will a man rob God?" You may be asking yourself, how can I afford to give to God when I am not able to meet my personal obligations and care for my children? Malachi challenges us to trust God to be faithful in meeting our day-to-day needs. God promises to, *"Open the windows of heaven and pour out a blessing that we would not have room enough to receive."*

I have two children left at home for whom I have primary responsibility. After my divorce, it was extremely difficult to make ends meet and care for the day-to-day needs of a family. I was often tempted to withhold tithing because I was on the verge of financial disaster. I decided to trust God and give my way out of poverty. Through this act of faith, God began to open up avenues where my creditors were willing to work with me. My employer also offered me extended hours. I've learned how to budget limited funds to prepare for the lean times. We've never missed meals, and I have the assurance from the Lord that blessings are on the horizon. Let me assure you that God is faithful in fulfilling all his promises of *"supplying all our needs according unto his riches in glory."*

Case B
You have just been diagnosed as having a rare disease. You had your life all planned out. Marriage, family, and financial security were included in these plans. You've analyzed your situation and have come to the conclusion that the future looks bleak.

Your doctors are optimistic that, with proper treatment, your chance of living a normal life is greatly enhanced. Sounds great, right? One drawback: You do not have medical coverage on your present job, and you have limited resources available. You find yourself greatly stressed because of the situation. What am I going to do, you're thinking? You are a believer, yet you feel hopeless about your situation.

There are many believers who feel that all sickness is not of God. Dear sister in the Lord, it is the will of God that we "prosper naturally and be in good health even as our spirit man (soul) prospers." The Lord holds each of us responsible to care properly for our bodies which he has wonderfully fashioned after his very image. Let's start with a proper diet. Certain foods high in fat, cholesterol, salt, and sugar work against the natural metabolism of our bodies and can lead to high blood pressure, strokes, and heart problems. If you have a tendency towards ill health, consultation with a nutritionist or a medical doctor is well advised. Incorporating nutrients, vitamins, iron, calcium, etc. into your daily diet is an excellent insurance against sickness. Further, adequate rest, approximately eight hours and proper exercise are also important deterrents to ill health.

What might the individual in Case B do to obtain medical attention? There are numerous local agencies within any state or town that can be of service to the individual. Checking with social services or private community assistance programs may prove beneficial.

A word of warning to any individual who preplans his or her life: Tomorrow is not guaranteed to anyone. Work on being all that God desires just one day at a time. Commit yourself to the safe keeping of Jesus, because He has a unique purpose for all of our lives. Even in sickness, your life can give Him the glory. Remember, through your faith, God can heal you.

Case C

Your twenty-year marriage is on the rocks. You realize that a Godly marriage counselor could offer helpful insights into working through your differences. The only drawback: Your mate refuses to seek help from outsiders.

It is unfortunate, but nevertheless true, divorce is on the upswing in our Christian communities. Divorce has never been the will of God except where adultery existed. When lines of communication have been severed for whatever reason, the home will not stand.

Divorce not only effects the husband and wife, but the children suffer as well. I believe with my whole heart that the family who incorporates worship, leisure, etc., together will weather any storm. Every marriage has its rocky moments, yet those mates who are first committed to God and then to each other will work on keeping communication alive.

Conclusion of the Matter

Problems that have no direct connection to an individual's life will appear easy to solve. If you have experienced one or more of the above cases, you will readily agree it is quite easy to become stressed, because any prolonged anxiety can take control over a person.

I realize the Bible says, *"In all of our ways to acknowledge him and he will direct our paths,"* yet how many of us really do this when we are faced with a difficult problem? If we are honest with ourselves, we spend countless hours trying to solve problems or look to others for answers, right?

If we would take the time to seek God first, our problems would lose their significance. We can then herald with confidence, *"I can do all things through Christ that strengthens me."* There is a song in my spirit that say, "Let Jesus fit it for you, he knows just what to do. Whenever you pray, let him have his way, and he will fix it for you."

Chapter Five
Mental and Physical Effects

Stress affects both our mental and physical capacities. Each year millions of Americans die of stress related illnesses. As discussed earlier, diseases such as heart problems, strokes, and high blood pressure are attributed to stress. Americans are slaves to prescribed medication to lower blood pressure and cholesterol and to regulate the heart. Besides the physical diseases associated with stress, there are several types of mental disorders and compulsive behaviors also associated with this condition.

Genesis 2:8 states, *"The Lord God formed man of the dust of the ground and breathed into his nostrils the breath of life, and man became a living soul and God saw that it was good."* Though our bodies are perfectly designed by God in his image, this does not exempt the Christian from attacks of anxiety and other disorders.

Warning Signs
Distinct warning signs are given before stress spirals out of control. Taking heed to these signs averts serious mental and physical breakdowns. When an infection, cold, or other illness attacks, symptoms such as a headache, fever, runny nose, or cough signals the onset of illness. These are the warning signs to treat the condition before it grows worse. Likewise, stress manifest itself outwardly in areas such as fatigue, restlessness, insomnia, short tempers, and headaches. The internal signs of stress are depression, feelings of escape, thoughts of suicide, or fear.

Stress can also lead to certain compulsive and addictive behaviors. Alcoholism, drug use, caffeine addiction, and eating disorders are byproducts of stress. Just as you would seek treatment for other major or minor physical illness, get help for stress.

Let Go of the Struggle
Have you noticed that when your body or mind is under attack it seems as if you can't find the right words to offer up in prayer? Romans 8:26 says, *"Likewise, the spirit also helpeth our infirmity; for we know not what we should pray as we ought; but the spirit himself maketh intercession for us with groans which cannot be uttered."*

Have you ever wrestled with the notion that maybe God is not concerned about what you are going through? Isaiah 43:2 answers, *"When thou passes through the waters, I will be with thee; when thou walketh through the fire, thou shalt not be burned, neither shalt the flames kindle upon thee."*

Have you ever felt you had received deliverance while in the assembly of other believers, only to discover later that your deliverance was short lived when the problem(s) resurfaced? The Bible says, *"That whom the Son set free, is free indeed."*

Have you ever tried to praise God in song, psalms, or dance, but your heart really was not in it? Psalms 34 is your assurance to praise God in spite of what you are faced with or how you might feel. Let his praises first be in your heart and then upon your lips. The Lord is near unto those who are broken hearted. He will deliver the faint hearted out of all their troubles and affiliations as they began to offer up praise.

Getting the Help You Need
Those who suffer from the effects of prolonged mental stress should seek professional help. A qualified minister of the gospel or other mental health care specialists can give this help. They should be sensitive to your needs and sensitive to the leading of the Lord. Some may disagree with receiving care from a health care specialist, but many churches have born again believers who are in this field. Not only will they use the skills of their respective field, but many will also give you spiritual counseling and prayer.

Before any treatment can be effective, the individual must first be willing to admit they have a problem that may or may not be obvious. Second, the individual must be willing to develop trust in the specialist that is providing the help.

Airing internal hurts can place the person at a disadvantage where they are open to scrutiny, criticism, and more hurts by others. This may be a very difficult time for some to open up and trust others with their personal feelings. Feelings of shame, reproach, or fear of what others may say or feel is a hurdle that you can overcome. Put these feelings behind you and get the help you need. The sooner you let go of whatever is causing you discomfort, the sooner the healing can begin.

No More Excuses
Romans 8:35 says, *"What shall separate you from the love of LORD? Shall trouble or hardship or persecution or famine or nakedness or danger or sword?"* Denying or avoiding the problem is not an effective way to handle stress. Likewise, when you blame yourself, others, or God, this hinders the healing process. The only way to overcome every excuse of bitterness, self pity, resentment, or depression in your life is to yield every stressful situation unto the Lord.

You may even be an individual who has ministered to others hurts or needs, yet there seems to be no hope for your own problems. Let me give you some encouragement for the moment you may be pressed on all sides: Hold on. Help from heaven is on its way. The Lord is speaking to you right now, saying, "I am here to bind up your broken heart and to completely heal your emotions."

Healing the Emotions
Many problems of a personal nature, such as rebellious children or a troubled marriage, may be harder to let go. These types of problems tend to affect the emotions because of personal commitments to spouse and children. After praying earnestly for God to fix the situation(s), don't pick up these cares again.

As with any stressful situation, prayer should first be made for the healing of your own emotions and then others. As you yield your emotions, the miraculous power of God will change how you perceive the problem. God works on the attitudes so that your reactions to others reflect peace and not confusion. The Bible says, "God is not the author of confusion." Further, *"we are to follow peace with all men."* Ask God *to create within you a clean heart and renew a right spirit within you.*

Inner healing is a process of time that requires you to surrender to God's purpose for your life. It excludes your right to reclaim hurts or take on new ones. It requires you to declare unto yourself, I am healed by the wounds placed in Jesus's sides for all my hangups. God can change your negative outlook on life. With a renewed attitude and yielded emotions, you can find peace in the midst of all your trials.

Chapter Six
Spiritual Warfare

<u>Characteristic and Plan of the Enemy</u>
Ephesians 6:11–12 says, *"Put on the whole armor of God, that ye may be able to stand against the wiles of the evil one. For we wrestle not against flesh and blood, but against the rulers of the darkness of this world, against spiritual wickedness in high places."*

These passages of Scripture describe the believer's unseen enemy. They also emphasize the need to be spiritually prepared to stand against every tactic of the enemy. Satan's master plan is to get the believer to deny God's Word in mind and then in action. Fighting spiritual warfare is an area where the believer must know whom they are in Lord. They must also be armed with the Word of God. God has decreed that *"whatever you bind on earth, he would bind in heaven."*

Our adversary is a master of deception. He uses things, individuals, and even your own beliefs and attitude to fight against the emotions. The adversary is skilled at hiding the real intent of the battle behind a camouflage that creates fear in the mind of the believer. The Word of God declares that those things hidden will be made manifest in the light. Psalms 23 stresses reliance on the shepherdship of the Lord to lead the believer through *"The valley of the shadow of death"* where there is no fear of evil.

The adversary is well acquainted with your weaknesses and strengths. Because our enemy is a spirit, he uses human vehicles through which to wage his battle. He realizes that if he uses those close to us, such as our children, or husbands, or even friends, this will create confusion and shame in our lives.

Those of you who are under attack right now, the spirit of the Lord says, "As you seek me in fellowship, I will undercover the plan of the enemy. I have given you power over every unclean spirit to bind and cast down in my name, saith the Lord."

The Bible describes the various characteristics of satan's nature as *a "roaring lion who walketh about seeking whom he may devour."* We are instructed to be sober and vigilant. Sober implies a steadfast mind whereas vigilant implies watch fullness or alert to danger. Satan can become an angel of light whenever he wants to deceive God's people. The Bible gives us to know, if it were possible, he could deceive the very elect. You have the spirit of God within you to try every spirit by the spirit of the Holy Ghost.

Our weapon of the Word of God is effective in fighting against every wile of the devil. Since we are more than conquerors, we cannot afford to become a casualty. There is no room for compromising; we are biblically instructed *"not to be conformed to this world but to be transformed by the renewing of the mind."* The devil has come against you to steal, kill, and to destroy your joy, hope, and your faith. Your victory is knowing that *the "Lord is your light and salvation, who shall you fear, the Lord is the strength of your life, of whom shall you be afraid, when you enemies, even your foes come upon you to eat of your flesh they shall stumble and fall. Though a host should encamp against you, in this will you are confident."*

Satan's attacks are without regard to the believer's maturity level in God. His battle ground is the mind of the believer. Each spiritual level you grow into there are new demonic forces with which to contend. Every believer is assigned tormenting spirit(s) by satan. Your decision *to "fight the good fight of faith, to lay hold of eternal life"* has placed you on the devil's hit list. You cannot afford to become stressed out in the heat of the battle. *"The race is not given to the swift nor the battle to the mighty, but to those that endure until the end."*

Knowing who they are in Christ is important for the believer. You have the authority in Jesus's name to cast down every imagination and stressful thought that attacks the mind. Heaven promises to back you up; *"Whatever you bind on earth shall be bound in heaven. Whatever you loose on earth, shall be loosed in heaven."*

Case Problem

Suppose you are a single mother with two teenage children. Lately it seems as if the children are more rebellious. You are not sure, but you have a feeling your son is using drugs; your daughter will not follow your request to be at home by a certain time. The peace that was once in your home is just not there. Other areas of your life seem out of order also. You are at wit's end on how to restore unity within your home. You are unable to sleep at night. Each time you hear a siren, you worry it may be one of your children. You can't figure out what went wrong. You love the Lord with all your heart. You are very faithful to the ministry. Why this trouble, oh Lord, you pray each day? This case could be anyone, anywhere in the world. You are under satanic attack. Satan looks for every possible avenue to enter. If he cannot use you, he then uses those that are close to us to vex our spirits. In order for satan to manipulate your life, there must be some area you are spiritually forsaking. Examples might include: Forsaking to include your children in daily devotion. It is important that children attend God's house whether it's popular or not. If this case is similar to your situation, begin now anointing your house, children, and yourself. Demand that demon, in Jesus's name, to leave. Each morning before the children leave for school, anoint them and cover them in the blood of Jesus.

You Are Not Alone in the Battle
An earlier chapter discussed attack by satan as very stressful. Job experienced all the classic symptoms you and I are familiar with—illness, despair, financial woes, and depression. From his seemly bleak situation, Job's spirit man rose and declared that God had given all and he could take all. He blessed God and sinned not with his mouth. Though the time is not stated, I believe Job's trial lasted a long time. Yet at the time appointed by God, Job was blessed more than the beginning of his life. The Word of God promises that all that the cankerworm (destroyer) has eaten he shall return seven folds.

The Apostle Paul was also familiar with stress. He spoke of how he was distressed often. He was shipwrecked, beaten without cause, thrown in prison, and lacked the necessities of life. Like Job, he firmly fixed his hope in God. In Phillippines 4:12 he declared, *"I know what it is to be in need and, I know what it is to have plenty. I have learned the secret of being content in any situation, whether well fed or hungry, whether living in plenty or in want. I can do everything through him who gives me strength."* Let this be your testimony as well.

I want to encourage the weary or faint hearted who feel their lives are filled with nothing but prolonged attacks. Ecclesiastes 3:1 advises, *"to everything there is a season, and a time to every purpose under the heaven."* There is a time for the good things of life and there is a time when life has its sorrows. At this present moment it may be your time of trouble. Don't give up. God shall work it out for your good. What the enemy purposed to cause you stress shall turn to the good. Though you may be in the wilderness of your life, you shall make it. Speak the words of life to your situation.

Chapter Seven
Soaring Above the Enemy

Before a soldier is declared battlefield ready, the soldier is subjected to tactical warfare training. Part of the soldier's training includes briefing on the characteristics of the enemy. The Bible gives the characteristics of our enemy as a lion who lurks about seeking out unsuspecting weaken souls to devour.

When we ignore the signs of stress, we open the door to attack because of our weaken emotional state. Our best defense against attack is to gird up the mind in prayer and fasting. We must also, change our negative way of thinking and spend time in the Word of God.

I have compiled a non-exclusive list of areas stress can vent into if allowed to go unchecked.

COMMON DEMON GROUPINGS

Bitterness
Resentment
Hatred
Unforgiveness
Violence
Temper
Anger
Retaliation
Murder

Retaliation
Destruction
Spite
Hatred
Sadism
Hurt
Cruelty

Accusation
Judging
Criticism
Fault Finding

Insecurity
Inferiority
Self-pity
Loneliness
Timidity
Shyness
Inadequacy
Ineptness

Rejection
Fear of Rejection
Self-rejection

Rebellion
Self-will
Stubbornness
Disobedient
Anti-submissiveness

Strife
Bickering
Argument
Quarreling
Fighting

Control
Possessiveness
Dominance
Witchcraft

Jealousy
Envy
Suspicion
Distrust
Selfishness

Withdrawal
Pouting
Daydreaming
Fantasy
Unreality

Escape
Indifference
Stoicism
Passivity
Sleepiness

Alcohol
Drugs

Passivity
Indifference
Listlessness
Lethargy

Depression
Despair
Despondency
Discouragement
Defeatism
Dejection
Hopelessness
Suicide
Death
Insomnia
Morbidity

Heaviness
Gloom
Burden
Disgust

These areas can become demonic strongholds that only the power of God can destroy. Prayerfully examine this list, then seek the Lord to reveal areas in your life where satan may be holding you hostage. Regardless of the pressures coming against you at this moment, you have the plan of escape. As a born again believer, you have been given the status of "conqueror," which implies victory over the silent enemy.

Personal Warfare

In teaching and counseling women of all ages, I have discovered that many are perplexed about how to tactfully handle stressful situations. Many want to bring about a peaceful resolution. The natural tendency is to fight "fire with fire." You may gain superficial peace, but the end result is a strained relationship. In the Bible we are instructed to "follow peace with everyone." Further, a "soft answer turns away wrath." Be willing, as an ambassador of Christ, to go the extra mile for peace sake. In doing so, you have gained the victory and stilled the silent enemy.

Case Problem

Let's examine a situation that is obviously stressful. Picture yourself as a character in this story. How can you gain the victory when the odds appear stacked against you? You pray yet somehow your answer is hindered. What is your duty to maintain this relationship?

In this relationship, your mate has an uncontrollable temper, which often explodes into violence. You are feeling stressed out; sleepless nights are common. Lately you find yourself withdrawing from friends and family. You ask yourself, what have I done to deserve such treatment? When not feeling sorry for yourself, you are also depressed and angry. Your mate apologizes after his tantrums, yet you are finding it hard to forgive. You feel that your hope of sanity is to abandon the marriage.

Not only are you stressed out, which you are denying, but bitterness, withdrawal, insecurity, depression, and strife are now a part of your life.

In this scenario, stress obscures victory. Divorce, which is at an all time high even in the Christian community, may appear a welcomed solution. Yet, in 1 Corinthians 7:10-11 it states: *"To the married I give this command (not I, but the Lord); a wife must not separate from her husband." Nevertheless, if she does, she must remain unmarried or else be reconciled to her husband."*

To battered and stressed out wives, this does not appear a workable solution on the surface. Let's examine this Scripture closely. The implication is to work out your unreconcilable differences through coming together as a family unit. You must admit some problems exist, seek spiritual counseling, and incorporate prayer. If, and only if, efforts to reconcile do not work, then the Scripture gives a way out by allowing separation. Separation should be used as the cooling off period. The mate who is experiencing the violent temper should seek help to decide the root cause which may be health related or even demonic. The battered mate must also seek help.

I strongly feel that there is a demonic attack on the Christian family. When the Christian home suffers extreme stress from whatever the source, the church is going to feel the effects. The greatest resource the family has is to fortify its ties with prayer, communication, and corporate devotion on a regular basis.

Resources to Victory
The conquerors resources lie not only in knowing the characteristics of the enemy, but also familiarity with spiritual weaponry. When backed into the corner of lack, despair, bankruptcy, desertion, or ill health, your unfailing weapons unfold on the pages of the Word of God. He promised never to desert you in your hour of need, to supply all needs according to his riches in glory. The Lord's desire is that you prosper naturally and have good health as your soul prospers. The Lord instructed us not to worry about our life, what we would eat or drink, or our clothing. If the Lord is able to care for nature in all its splendor and provide for the animals of the forest, he is very capable of meeting the needs of man who is created in his image.

When our sufficiency is in self, we actually open our flood gates to greater spiritual attacks. In the book of Ephesians 6:10–11, the following instructions are given: *"Be strong in the Lord and in his mighty power. Put on the full armor of God so that you can take your stand against the devil's schemes. Therefore, put on the full armor of God, so that when the day of evil comes, you may be able to stand your ground."* Your weapons include: *"The belt of truth, the breastplate of righteousness, and with your feet fitted with the readiness that comes from the gospel of peace. Further, take the shield of faith, with which you can extinguish all the flaming arrows of the evil one. Take the helmet of salvation and the sword of the spirit which is the Word of God."* Ephesians 6:14–17).

Chapter Eight
Challenges of the Ministry

Challenges to Our Faith
This chapter is dedicated to both lay and ministering women whose families face challenges to their faith.

This is a very touchy area to discuss. Nevertheless, I feel led of the Lord to address stress issues facing the Christian woman in ministries. I realize that there are those who hold fast to the notion that sin or some shortcoming exists when Christians boldly own up to suffering from stress or other physical illness. It is the will of God that your life be victorious even when faced with challenges that may not be pleasant.

Take a serious moment and evaluate your own day-to-day lifestyle. What did you discover? Are you faced with demands to balance your obligations toward the family unit, career, and God? As Godly women your main concern, outside love and service to the Lord, should be for the care and upkeep of your home. You should never neglect your duties toward your husband or children. I realize that because of economic pressures, many women must help support the family. The Scripture states that *"Holy women should be chase keepers at home, discreet, good, obedient to their own husbands, that the Word of God be not blasphemed."*

The Word of God in Psalms 1 says: *"...But his delight is in the Law of the Lord; and in his law doth he mediate day and night. And he shall be like a tree planted by the rivers of water, that bringeth forth its fruit in its season; its leaf also shall not wither; and whatsoever he doeth shall prosper."* Many unforeseen pressures attack the average woman each day. For example, just when you were about to spend some quite time in devotion with the Lord, something else distracted your attention; John fell and needs reassurance; the phone rang and the matter must be attended to immediately; or family or friends call upon you to handle a situation that was pressing on your time. As discussed in an earlier chapter, you must prayerfully set priorities in your life. Knowing when to say "no" to outsiders is a virtue you need to develop when requests are imposed upon you that places your own home in an uproar.

To those women do not have a mate, have you ever experienced having your back pressed against the wall of life? You just could not make ends meet. There isn't a husband to help with the children or to talk problems over. When you tried to pray, you felt as if the Lord was not there. You knew the Bible said, *"Lo, I am with you always,"* yet you could not feel his presence. Have you noticed that during these times you do not feel saved? This is the time you must press to obey the Bible in not forsaking the assembling of yourself with other believers. Strength is gained in coming together with other believers. You are also able to minister unto the Lord while the testimonies and encouragements of others minister unto your spiritual and natural needs.

In an earlier chapter, I suggested that if during your day you feel you are not able to fit time alone with God, arise early in the morning or spend time when everyone has retired for the evening. The enemy is going to fight your efforts; nevertheless, preserve—for in doing so you shall receive the help you need from God.

Take this time to reverence the Lord for being a very present help in all your situations. You can feel free to cast all your cares, hurts, and desires before the throne of God and leave them there. You can minister unto the Lord the promises contained in his Word for your life. It is in his presence, O women of God, that you shall find peace like a river. Every yoke of depression, worry, doubt, etc., can be cast down in his name.

Ministers And Evangelists

The Bible instructs us that a wise woman will build her house, but a fool will pluck it down with her hands. A true woman of God will not only be concerned about the ministry, but her own home. The ministry begins in her home and requires her undivided attention. Proverbs 3:10–30 portrays a virtuous woman (lay or minister), who cares for her family with diligence. She looks well to the ways of her household and eateth not the bread of idleness.

To those women who minister the gospel, there is double pressure on your lives to preach as well as maintain a balanced family life. Ministering the gospel requires that we spend an adequate amount of time alone in prayer, fasting, and study. If you are not knowledgeable about time management, other areas of your personal life will suffer tremendously. Let's look at a proposal. Set time aside to prayerfully develop a time schedule for your daily, personal, and professional life. This schedule must be one with which most of your family members can live. Try to solicit help with chores, shopping and running errands from all family members. This means that you must release responsibility to other capable hands for those activities you previously deemed your's alone.

Your schedule should include time for the family to come together in devotion and worship. I strongly believe that a family who prays together will stay together.

Time Out
The drudgery of day-to-day routines can cause tension in the home. As a vent, try to include fun outings and vacations into the family schedule. Rest and relaxation should be an integral part of your life. The Lord expects each individual to care for our wonderfully made bodies and minds.

The ministry requires patience and long suffering with individuals whose spiritual walks range from babes to mature adults and also those whose temperaments range from humble to rebellious. When your own life is filled with stress, it is next to impossible to be an effective minister.

Joel 2:28 and 20 states, *"And afterward, I will pour out my spirit on all people. Your sons and daughters will prophesy... Even on my servants, both men and women, I will pour out my spirit in those days.* This passage gives a glorious outlook on the outpouring of the Holy Spirit upon all flesh as fulfilled in Acts. Its implication is that the Holy Spirit will make both male and female effective ministers of the gospel. In Christ Jesus, there is no respect of persons.

As women of God, it is imperative that you hold fast the calling on your life. Never allow yourself to compromise the gospel despite the pressures imposed by those who feel women should not preach the gospel. The Lord holds each of us responsible to him alone for the stewardship he has entrusted to us.

The work of the ministry at times will be lonely and pressing, and at times disappointments will come. Nevertheless there is a reward if we hold fast the profession of our faith in which we are called as able ministers of the Lord Jesus Christ.

Your heavenly credentials came when you responded to the call of God. It is he alone who signs the approval on your life through justification and glorification. Your requirement is to meditate in the Word of God day and night, to be thoroughly equipped to preach the gospel in season and out of a season, in love despite the pressures you face.

Chapter Nine
Problem to Recovery

"...He hath sent me to bind up the brokenhearted, to proclaim liberty to the captives and the opening of the prison to those who are bound." Is. 61:1 (KJV)

Recently I saw a commercial for a hospital that offered counseling to persons suffering from stress and other oppressive disorders. However equipped to serve the hurting, these professionals are not able to guarantee the patient "100 percent" recovery. The patients' only hope is to learn how to live a full life with the ever present threat of a relapse. I do not want to belittle the efforts of qualified clinical professionals. I believe they sincerely seek to help those incapable of freeing themselves from undesirable behaviors and thoughts. Despite their earnest intentions, the professionals' efforts are limited by what the sufferer is willing to confide or release.

It's refreshing to know we have an eternal doctor whose professional touch is not limited by our emotional hangups. The Lord knows you better than you then you know yourself. He is well acquainted with grief and suffering. The Lord cares about your total well being. The prescription is simple: *"Cast all you cares upon him for he careth for you."* This means release the right to hold on to all stressful hurts of the past or present.

Avenues of Hindrances
Self-pity and unforgiveness are areas that hinder healing and prevent individuals from going forward with their lives. Many never seem to lift themselves above memories of divorce, fear, anxiety, or depression. Doors in the individual's spiritual lives are opened to demonic strongholds that torment every thought.

There are many passages of scriptures to support our need to forgive. Mark 11:25–26 (KJV) says, *"And when ye stand praying, forgive, if ye have anything against any, that your Father also, who is in heaven may forgive you your trespasses. Nevertheless, if ye do not forgive, neither will your Father, who is in heaven, forgive your trespasses."* Another passage of Scripture instructs the believer to leave their gift at the altar and seek forgiveness first.

Learn How to Forgive
Forgiving frees one from bondage. Hurts of the past or present lose their significance when the individual forgives, whether they caused the incident(s) or not. Forgiving humbles the attitude because you first forgive yourself and then others. Forgiving acknowledges that God holds each of us responsible for how we treat others. Once forgiveness has taken place, don't look back; press forward toward the plan that God has ordained for your life.

Isaiah 42:9 points toward the bright future God has in store just for you: *"Behold, the former things are come to pass, and new things do I declare; before they spring forth I tell you of them."* Isaiah 43:19 continues, *"Behold, I will do a new thing; now it shall spring forth; shall ye not know it? I will even make a sway in the wilderness, and rivers in the desert."*

Instead of weeping and feeling sorry for yourself lift up your hands and begin to sing. Singing songs of victory and praise ushers in the presence of God. He understands every hurt you have suffered. He was *"bruised for your iniquity and the chastisement of your peace was upon him and by his stripes you are healed."* God is going to apply his balm of love to every wound. Where you were not fruitful, you can now be all that God requires. No longer will you have to be afraid. You will not suffer shame, fear or disgrace. God shall restore your honor.

Practical Insights
When your body and mind begin to show signs of stress, you should call time out. You cannot handle the present situation—so let God do it. Why is it necessary to call mental and, when necessary, physical time out? Because making sound decisions when in a mental overload state is impossible. Take this moment to fill your bath tub with hot water, add some sort of bubble bath and sea salt, fix yourself an enjoyable hot cup of herbal tea, relax and talk to God. He is never busy, and he is just waiting to hear from you. What you need immediately is peace of mind. Isaiah 26:3 says, *"Thou shalt keep him in perfect peace whose mind is stayed on thee, because he trusted in thee."* The Lord is able to work out the problem(s), no matter how complex. Problem solving avenues closed to you because of your limited knowledge are just opportunities for God to show his mercy and compassion.

When the Lord speaks a word of peace to a turbulent situation, *"His word that goeth forth out of his mouth does not return unto him void, but it shall accomplish that which he please, and shall prosper in the thing whereto he sent it."* Let God speak a word of peace toward you.

The first stage of recovery begins with the individuals willingness to allow the Lord to overhaul (cast down) negative thinking. *Jesus became the great high priest who could be touched with the feeling of our infirmities, for he himself was in all points tempted like as we are, yet without sin* (Hebrews 4:16) (KJV). Every born again believer has been given the right of access by prayer and supplication to the throne room of God. Hebrews 4:16 (KJV) states: *"Let us, therefore, come boldly unto the throne of grace, that we may obtain mercy, and find grace to help in time of need.* The Bible instructs us to *"cast down imaginations, and every high thing that exalts itself against the knowledge of God, and bringing into captivity every thought to the obedience of Christ."* The words "cast down" imply to resist or rebuke in the name of Jesus every thought that breeds self pity, anger, despair, etc. To be in "captivity" implies yielding to God's healing touch by thinking on what is good, pure, honest and of good report.

The words we speak have power to create life or death in any situation. Instead of saying, I can't make it; stand on the Word of God and declare, *"I can do all things through Christ that strengthens me."* Our limited resources do not indicate heaven is broke. *"Therefore, be not anxious saying, what shall we eat? Or what, what shall we drink? Or, with what shall we be clothed?...For your heavenly Father knoweth that ye have need of all these things."* There are times when you are going to feel the walls that the enemy of your soul has erected to hinder you from accomplishing what God has purposed for your life. David the Patriot declared that he would *"Look unto the hills from whence come his help."* David testified in the Fortieth Division of Psalms that, *"I waited patiently for the Lord, and he inclined unto me, and heart my cry. He brought me up also out of a horrible pit, out of the miry clay, and set my feet upon a rock, and established my goings. (KJV)"*

You Have the Answer

Please note that in previous chapters I have offered many insights to relieve stress including exercise, proper diet, health, and time management. When was the last time you took a vacation or just put all those things you thought were important to accomplish in the course of a day on hold and just relaxed? I want to encourage you to invest in a journal. Your first task will be to list those activities you perform during the day or week. After reviewing your list, does it afford you time out? Can these tasks be delegated? Now revise your list. Try to include fun activities in which you desire to get involved but never seem to have the time. Your final task is to prepare a time management schedule that would afford you time out during the week. I have prepared a sample schedule below—try to look for areas where this schedule might be revised:

TIME MANAGEMENT SCHEDULE

TASK	START TIME	TIME TASK COMPLETED	NOTES
Shower/breakfast	6:00 A.M.		
Occupation	8:00 A.M.	4:00 P.M.	8 hour day
Grocery shopping/errands	4:30 P.M.	5:30 P.M.	every two weeks
Prepare dinner	6:00 P.M.	8:30 P.M.	
T.V.	9:00 P.M.		

Before you start revision on the above schedule, prayerfully seek the Lord's guidance. It is important that adequate time be given for personal rest and time out as well as family devotion and recreation. Let me offer some suggestions: Try rising one-half hour earlier each morning for devotion and, if possible, exercise. Instead of taking total responsibility for errands and grocery shopping, solicit family members' help. Dinner preparation could also be a shared task. Just as a suggestion, you might prepare meals ahead of time and freeze them. An occasional family night out to dinner is a great opportunity to promote communication. Instead of the time spent in front of the television, it could well be spent together as a family.